Life As ...

Life As an Ambulance Driver in World War I

Laura L. Sullivan

New York

Published in 2018 by Cavendish Square Publishing, LLC
243 5th Avenue, Suite 136, New York, NY 10016

First Edition

Library of Congress Cataloging-in-Publication Data

Names: Sullivan, Laura L., 1974- author.
Title: Life as an ambulance driver in World War I / Laura L. Sullivan.
Description: New York : Cavendish Square Publishing, [2018] |
Series: Life as ... | Includes index.
Identifiers: LCCN 2017020183 (print) | LCCN 2017020462 (ebook) |
ISBN 9781502630575 (E-book) | ISBN 9781502630551 (pbk.) |
ISBN 9781502630568 (library bound) | ISBN 9781502632104 (6 pack)
Subjects: LCSH: World War, 1914-1918--Medical care--United States--Juvenile literature. | Ambulance drivers--Juvenile literature. | American Field Service--Juvenile literature. | United States. Army--Ambulances--Juvenile literature.
Classification: LCC D629.U6 (ebook) | LCC D629.U6 S85 2018 (print) |
DDC 940.54/7530973--dc23
LC record available at https://lccn.loc.gov/2017020183

Editorial Director: David McNamara
Editor: Kristen Susienka
Copy Editor: Rebecca Rohan
Associate Art Director: Amy Greenan
Designer: Lindsey Auten
Production Coordinator: Karol Szymczuk
Photo Research: J8 Media

The photographs in this book are used by permission and through the courtesy of: Cover Glen Jones/Shutterstock.com; p. 5 Topical Press Agency/Getty Images; p. 6 Everett Historical/Shutterstock.com; p. 8 Hulton Archive/Getty Images; p. 10 Hulton Archive/Getty Images; p. 13 Douglas Miller/Topical Press Agency/Getty Images; p. 14 Scott Carruthers/Alamy Stock Photo; p. 16 Lt. Ernest Brooks/IWM via Getty Images; p. 18 Paul Thompson/FPG/Getty Images; p. 20 Car Culture ® Collection/Getty Images; p. 22 wyrdlight/Alamy Stock Photo; p. 24 Photo Researchers/Science Source/Getty Images; p. 26 Oxford Science Archive/Print Collector/Getty Images.

Printed in the United States of America

Contents

Introduction

World War I (1914–1918) was a huge conflict that caused millions of deaths and injuries. While soldiers were fighting each other, an army of doctors, nurses, and ambulance drivers were trying to help the wounded. Ambulance drivers were very important to both sides. They carried injured soldiers to field hospitals. Once victims were away from the fighting and muddy **trenches**, they had a better chance of survival.

Cars and trucks were still relatively new and uncommon during that time. Not long before, mule-drawn carts were used to evacuate injured soldiers. In World War I, many animals were replaced by motorized ambulances. Many of the drivers were volunteers. They risked their lives to get wounded soldiers to safety.

Men and women worked hard to bring the wounded to hospitals during World War I.

Soldiers fought in muddy, bloody trenches during World War I. Here, Canadian troops go over the top of a trench and into battle.

Chapter 1

War Breaks Out

World War I was a global war that saw thirty-two countries battling. On the Allied side, the main nations were France, Britain, the United States, Russia, and Italy. They fought the Central Powers, which included Germany, the Ottoman Empire, and Austria-Hungary. The war lasted from July 28, 1914, to November 11, 1918. It began with the assassination of the Austrian archduke Franz Ferdinand by a Serbian. This led Austria-Hungary to declare war on Serbia. Other countries that had alliances with these two nations soon entered the war.

Also known as the Great War or the War to End All Wars, World War I was a long and bloody conflict. There were about thirty-eight million **casualties** of

Gas masks protected soldiers from deadly chemicals used in battle.

both the military and civilians. That includes more than twenty million wounded, and more than seventeen million killed.

World War I introduced a new kind of fighting. **Artillery** had become much more powerful. Now

US Enters the War

At the start of the war, the United States wanted to remain neutral. In 1917, though, German submarines sank five US merchant ships that were heading to Britain. Also, Germany tried to convince Mexico to join the war on their side. These two incidents outraged the United States and led it to enter the war on the Allied side on April 6, 1917.

soldiers had machine guns, flame throwers, poison gas, tanks, and airplanes. Fighters practiced trench warfare to defend against the new weaponry. They hunkered down in long lines of muddy trenches. Barbed wire and land mines covered the area between trenches, called "no-man's land." Soldiers received terrible injuries in this kind of fighting.

During the war era, cars were new and exciting. Many young men wanted jobs that involved driving them, including ambulance driving.

Chapter 2

Developing Ambulance Driving

Though the United States did not enter World War I right away, many US citizens wanted to show their support for England and France. Some sent money; some organized aid and relief. Others volunteered to go directly to the front. Since the United States wasn't in the war, they didn't usually fight. However, they could help the war effort in other ways, such as being part of vital medical teams. American doctors and nurses went to Europe. So did hundreds of people who volunteered as ambulance drivers.

Before World War I, ambulances and their drivers often had a bad reputation. Horse- or mule-drawn wagons were slow and bumpy, and carried no medical supplies. Patients were so jostled that the ride itself

Cars and Careers

Cars were so new and impressive that it became acceptable for educated or upper-class people to drive ambulances. In fact, of the 2,500 drivers who volunteered for the American Field Service at the start of the war, 859 were from the Ivy League universities Cornell, Harvard, Princeton, and Yale.

might kill them. Civilian (nonmilitary) drivers weren't skilled or respected. In the American Civil War, they were described as "civilian drunkards and thieves who ran when they heard the guns." That changed in World War I.

Wealthy Americans such as the Vanderbilt family, the railroad tycoons, gave money to start the American volunteer ambulance services. The Ford Motor Company donated many of its Model T cars to serve as ambulances. Volunteer ambulance drivers went first to France and later to Belgium. There were many different

Joe Carstairs (*right*) volunteered for the Red Cross ambulance service. Here she drives a speedboat in 1930.

Joe Carstairs

Marion Barbara "Joe" Carstairs was the wealthy daughter of an American heiress and a Scottish soldier. She had a passion for cars, and in World War I, she volunteered as an ambulance driver. She helped save many wounded in France. After the war, she founded a chauffeur service staffed entirely by women and also became a champion powerboat racer.

ambulance units. The largest was the American Field Service (AFS). When the United States entered the war, the AFS had two thousand American volunteers.

This member of the First Aid Nursing Yeomanry wears old-fashioned garb as she sits on her horse.

Chapter 3

Being an Ambulance Driver

World War I gave different opportunities for women to get involved. When men joined to fight, women sometimes took the jobs they left at home. Other times, they filled vital noncombat roles at the front, such as ambulance driver.

The First Aid Nursing Yeomanry (FANY) was an all-female volunteer unit. When it started in 1907, the women rode horseback to get to the wounded in rough terrain. When World War I began, though, they switched to motorcars.

Even though they weren't supposed to be involved directly in the fighting, there was danger everywhere. The ambulance drivers raced along muddy, rutted

Women played a valuable part in World War I as ambulance drivers.

roads while shells exploded all around them. They were hurt by accidents on the bad roads or killed by gunfire. Although ambulances were not supposed to be targeted by either side, they weren't always safe in the confusion of battle. Many ambulance drivers were killed. The American Red Cross alone had 127 of its ambulance drivers killed.

Ambulance drivers saw gruesome injuries. It was the first war to use high-explosive bombs. **Shrapnel** tore off limbs and ripped off flesh. Because the soldiers fought in trenches, head injuries were very common, as they were the first parts exposed when a soldier peeked over the top. While medics tried to prevent blood loss and shock, ambulance drivers had to take the wounded to field hospitals where they could be properly treated.

In addition to injuries, many soldiers also got bad diseases. They fought in fields that had been fertilized with manure. The manure caused even small wounds to become easily infected. Diseases could sweep through a unit, killing many. World War I also saw the use of **chemical weapons**. These could severely damage lungs or kill whoever breathed it. Ambulance drivers had to face these terrible casualties and do their best to get people to safety and aid.

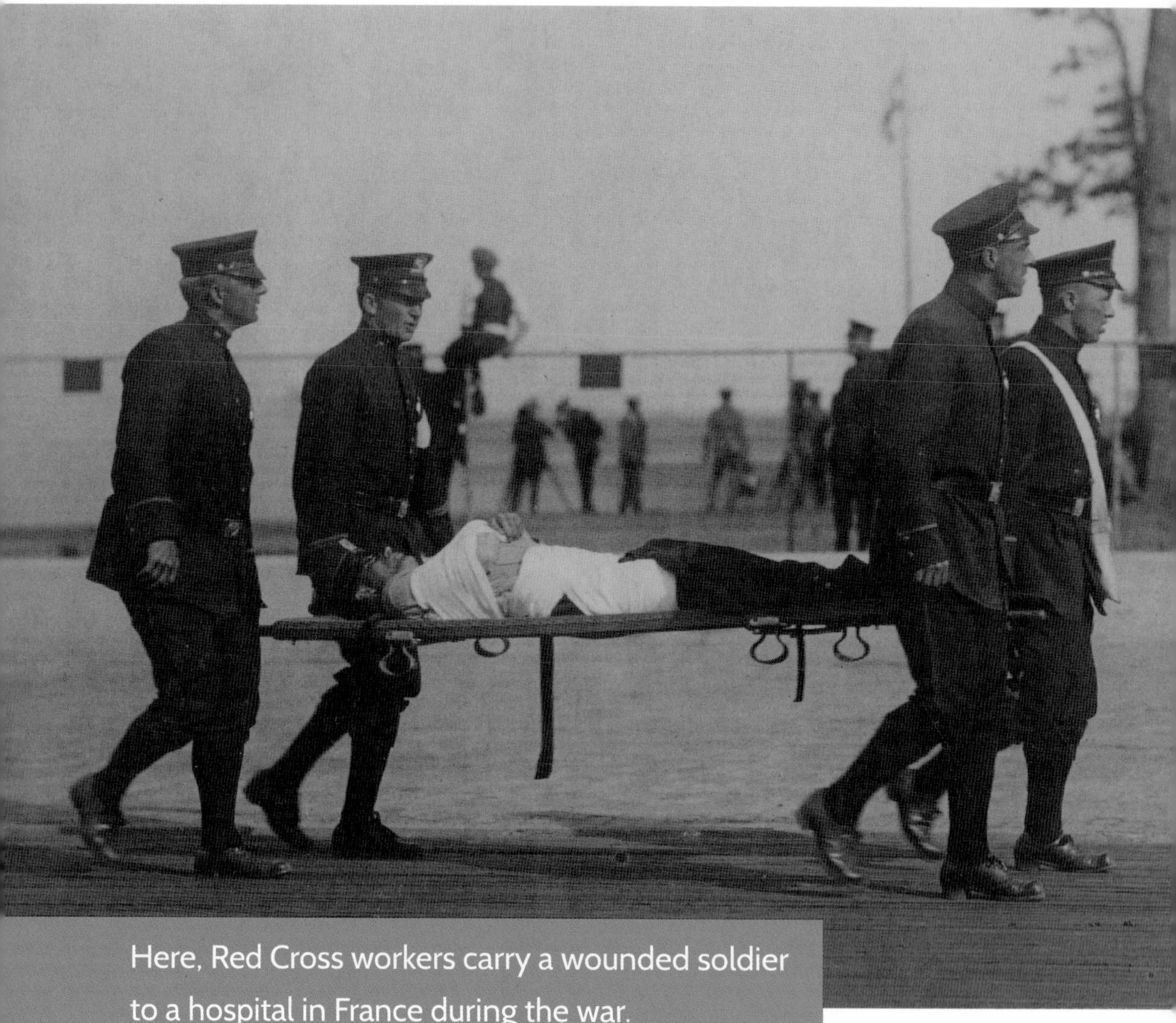

Here, Red Cross workers carry a wounded soldier to a hospital in France during the war.

An Ambulance Driver's Day

A driver's day could change, but this is what one might look like:

3:00 a.m.	Woken by enemy shelling.
5:00 a.m.	Check ambulance tires and engine. Fill tank with gas.
6:00–noon	Evacuate wounded soldiers from the front lines to a field hospital.
1:00–8:00 p.m.	Drive stable patients to a hospital in the nearest city.
9:00 p.m.	Siren signals gas attack. Put on gas mask and goggles. False alarm.
10:00 p.m.	Sleep in the garage, dressed and ready for the next call.

The inside of a Model T looked a little different than a modern car.

Chapter 4

Tools for Driving

Ford's Model T cars were the foundation of the World War I ambulance service. They were inexpensive, reliable, and easy to repair. They were also light. If a Model T got stuck in the mud, six or eight soldiers could pick it up by hand.

The Model T was strong. It was made with a steel alloy that could withstand rough use. It was also flexible. The frame was riveted rather than welded. That meant that the chassis, or frame, could move and bend a little bit without cracking when it was shaken by rough roads. The Model T could travel on very bad roads at 30 miles per hour (48 kilometers per hour). On good roads, it could reach about 42 miles per hour (68 kph).

The Model T Ford was the main car model used as an ambulance.

The body of the Model T ambulance was big enough to hold either three patients on stretchers or four seated patients. Another two patients could sit in the front next to the driver.

Another useful tool was developed by famed scientist and two-time Nobel Prize winner Marie Curie. When the war broke out, Curie realized she could put **X-ray** technology to use for the war effort. She convinced carmakers to convert vehicles into X-ray trucks. That way, doctors could find bullets, shrapnel, or broken bones in patients on the front line.

Curie learned to operate the X-ray machinery and also to drive so she could perform this service herself. She also taught her eighteen-year-old daughter Irène. Together, they went to the front, and both drove the X-ray ambulances. Curie later trained 150 women to do the same.

Zeppelin Attack

Ambulance drivers served on the home front in England, too. Germany sent zeppelins—huge hydrogen-filled, balloon-like airships—to bomb London. During the first serious attack, many people were hurt or killed. First on the scene was the Women's Reserve Ambulance unit. Though they had never before seen such injuries, they quickly loaded the injured into ambulances and took them to the hospital.

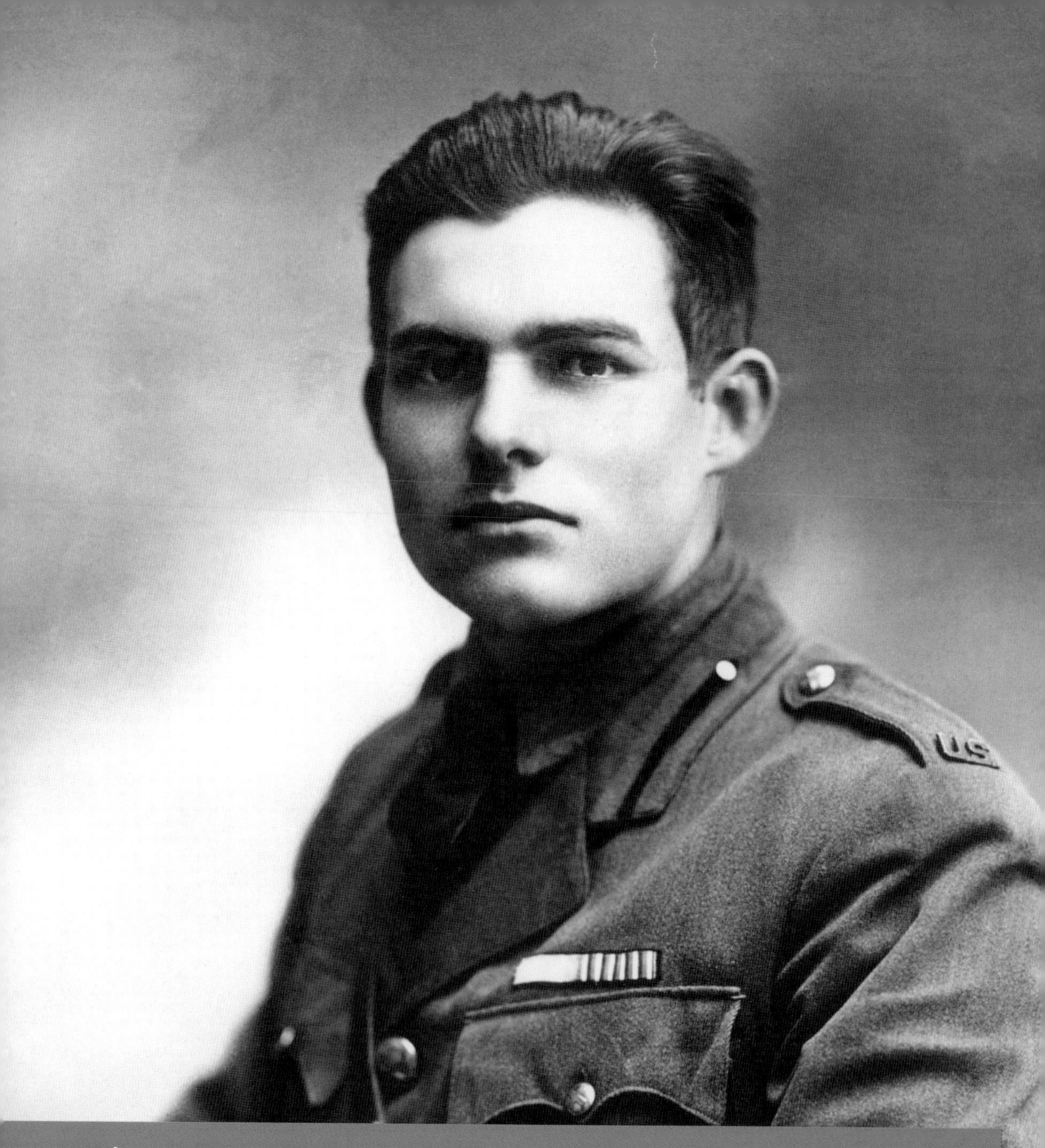

As a young man, writer Ernest Hemingway drove an ambulance in World War I. He later put some of his wartime experiences into his novels.

Chapter 5

Ambulance Driving Today

Though World War I was called the War to End All Wars, it wasn't. It was followed in 1939 by World War II. Many other conflicts came in later decades. In all of them, ambulance drivers provided crucial services.

During World War I, women proved that they were very capable ambulance drivers. As soon as World War II broke out, women started driving ambulances again. They served on the home front during bombing raids. They also worked close to the fighting. Ever since, women have participated in serving their countries.

In World War I, famous authors and poets such as e. e. cummings, Ernest Hemingway, and John Dos

Many women took pride in driving and taking care of their ambulances. After the war, women fought for more independence.

Passos became ambulance drivers. Authors were able to use their experience of the horrors of war in their work. Helping people see how terrible war can be might help avoid future wars.

Today, ambulance drivers are used around the world. They are not only used in combat but in everyday life. Ambulances bring people who need help to hospitals to get treated. The ambulance driver will be needed for generations to come.

A modern ambulance races to an emergency.

Glossary

artillery Large projectile-launching weapons used in combat. Machine guns, rockets, and cannons are some examples.

casualty A person who has either been injured or killed in a war or conflict.

chemical weapon A weapon that uses chemicals to cause damage; the chemicals can be inhaled or absorbed though the skin.

shrapnel Small pieces of a bomb or bullet that are scattered during an explosion.

trench A long, narrow ditch. In World War I, each side dug long trenches, from which they fought.

X-ray A kind of energy wave that can pass through some solid materials, allowing someone to see the inside.

Find Out More

Books

Atwood, Kathryn J. *Women Heroes of World War I: 16 Remarkable Resisters, Soldiers, Spies, and Medics.* Chicago, IL: Chicago Review Press, 2014.

Grant, R.G. *World War I: The Definitive Visual History*. New York: DK Publishing, 2014.

Website

BBC Schools – World War I

http://www.bbc.co.uk/schools/0/ww1

Video

Life in a Trench

http://www.history.com/topics/world-war-i/world-war-i-history/videos/life-in-a-trench

This History Channel video has reenactments and real photos of life in a World War I trench.

Index

Page numbers in **boldface** are illustrations. Entries in **boldface** are glossary terms.

About the Author

Laura L. Sullivan is the author of more than forty fiction and nonfiction books for children, including the fantasies *Under the Green Hill* and *Guardian of the Green Hill*. She lives in Florida, where she likes to swim, hike, canoe, hunt fossils, and practice Brazilian jiu-jitsu.